GROW YOUR MIND

DON'T PANIC

Written by Alice Harman
Illustrated by David Broadbent

CRABTREE
PUBLISHING COMPANY
WWW.CRABTREEBOOKS.COM

CRABTREE
PUBLISHING COMPANY
WWW.CRABTREEBOOKS.COM

Author: Alice Harman
Series designer: David Broadbent
Illustrator: David Broadbent
Editor: Crystal Sikkens
Proofreader: Melissa Boyce
Print coordinator: Katherine Berti

A trusted adult is a person (over 18 years old) in a child's life who makes them feel safe, comfortable, and supported. It might be a parent, teacher, family friend, social worker, or another adult.

Library and Archives Canada Cataloguing in Publication

Title: Don't panic / written by Alice Harman ; illustrated by David Broadbent.
Names: Harman, Alice, author. | Broadbent, David, 1977- illustrator.
Description: Series statement: Grow your mind | Includes index. |
  First published in Great Britain in 2020 by the
  Watts Publishing Group.
Identifiers: Canadiana (print) 20200219952 |
  Canadiana (ebook) 20200220586 |
  ISBN 9780778781684 (hardcover) |
  ISBN 9780778781769 (softcover) |
  ISBN 9781427125941 (HTML)
Subjects: LCSH: Panic attacks—Juvenile literature. | LCSH: Anxiety in
  children—Juvenile literature. | LCSH: Worry in children—Juvenile
  literature. | LCSH: Anxiety—Juvenile literature. | LCSH: Worry—
  Juvenile literature. | LCSH: Calmness—Juvenile literature.
Classification: LCC RC535 .H37 2021 | DDC j616.85/223—dc23

Library of Congress Cataloging-in-Publication Data

Names: Harman, Alice, author. | Broadbent, David, 1977- illustrator.
Title: Don't panic / written by Alice Harman ; illustrated by David Broadbent.
Description: Great Britain : The Watts Publishing Group ; New York, New
  York : Crabtree Publishing Company, [2020] | Series: Grow your mind |
  Includes index.
Identifiers: LCCN 2020015528 (print) |
  LCCN 2020015529 (ebook) |
  ISBN 9780778781684 (hardcover) |
  ISBN 9780778781769 (paperback) |
  ISBN 9781427125941 (ebook)
Subjects: LCSH: Worry in children--Juvenile literature.
Classification: LCC BF723.W67 H37 2020 (print) | LCC BF723.W67
  (ebook) | DDC 155.4/1246--dc23
LC record available at https://lccn.loc.gov/2020015528
LC ebook record available at https://lccn.loc.gov/2020015529

Crabtree Publishing Company

www.crabtreebooks.com   1-800-387-7650
Published by Crabtree Publishing Company in 2021

Published in Canada
Crabtree Publishing
616 Welland Ave.
St. Catharines, Ontario
L2M 5V6

Published in the United States
Crabtree Publishing
347 Fifth Ave.
Suite 1402-145
New York, NY 10116

Printed in the U.S.A./082020/CG20200601

First published in Great Britain in 2020 by The Watts Publishing
Group Copyright © The Watts Publishing Group 2020

CONTENTS

A calm mindset

Don't panic! It's easy to say, but it can be pretty tricky to stay calm sometimes, can't it?

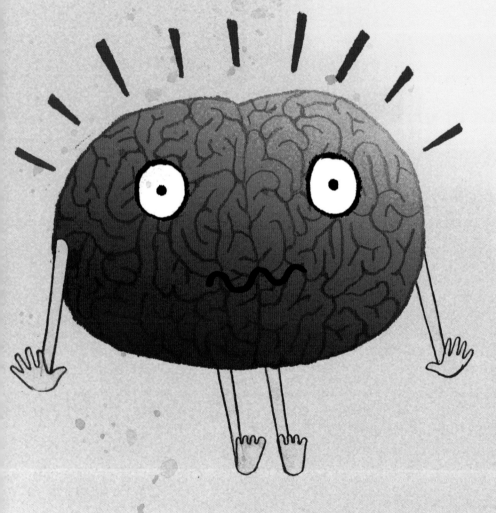

Nobody wants to panic. It's not a very nice feeling when your heart is pounding in your chest and your breathing becomes short and quick.

But when we feel like things are getting out of control and that we don't know how to fix them, our brains can sometimes switch into panic mode.

So what can we do to avoid panicking? It's not possible to never feel any stress at all, but there are all kinds of things we can do to prevent our worries from turning into full-blown panic.

You can help teach your brain to respond differently to stress and to react more calmly and positively when problems and difficult situations pop up in your life.

Sometimes we don't realize how much power we have to change our brains, because people often talk about them as if they're fixed. When using this **fixed mindset**, people believe someone is either smart or not, or that a person is either relaxed or a worrier.

If we switched our way of thinking to a **growth mindset**, we would realize that this is not true. Our brains are always changing and growing. We have billions of **neurons** in our brain that pass messages to one another. Our thoughts and actions can help build new neuron-connecting paths, as well as strengthen helpful ones that already exist.

This also means that if we feel like we can't do something, there's no need to panic. We can practice thinking and acting in ways that, over time, can help turn that "can't" into a "can"!

Future friend

One of the best ways to avoid getting stressed and panicking is by being a friend to your future self. But what exactly does that mean?

Well, here's an example. Imagine you are given homework on Friday that you have to hand in on Monday. You know you'll probably feel stressed and panicky on Sunday evening if you try to do it all in a hurry then. What could you do ahead of time to avoid that panic?

If your answer is "start on Friday or Saturday so I don't overload my brain trying to get it all done on Sunday," then you already have a pretty good idea of how to be a **future friend** to yourself!

It's all about understanding what might make you feel panicked in the future and doing what you can now to take away some of that pressure or fear.

Think of three situations that might make you feel panicked or that have made you feel that way in the past.

Some examples might include...

★ **Performing on stage in a school play**

★ **Not knowing what work you're supposed to be doing for a group project that's due tomorrow**

★ **Having to talk to kids you don't know at a new after-school or weekend activity**

What can you do ahead of time to be a future friend to yourself and make yourself feel more prepared and confident? Brainstorm with an adult to come up with some ideas for each situation, then circle the ideas you think might be most helpful and give them a try!

Nervous or excited?

Do you ever have a fluttery "butterflies in your stomach" feeling when you're really excited about something? Perhaps you have a pounding heartbeat in your chest? Maybe you get all fidgety, too, and find it hard to relax?

If you think about it, it's probably pretty similar to how you feel when you're nervous, right? That's because in both cases your body is releasing a substance called adrenaline, which gives you a burst of energy to help tackle whatever you're nervous or excited about.

We often think of being nervous as a bad thing, but it can be a sign that something is important to you and you want it to go well. Instead of thinking, "Oh no, I'm really nervous about this," you could say to yourself, "Oh wow, I'm really excited about this!"

The more you practice thinking positively, the easier it gets for your brain to do it. So let's get practicing...

1. Write down what's making you feel nervous. Around it, write or draw what you're worried might happen.

2. Cross through each worry, replacing it with something you're excited about that might happen. Then add some actions you could take to help make this positive outcome a reality.

For example, if you're starting at a new school, you might be nervous about not knowing anyone. A more positive view could be that you're excited about the opportunity to make new friends, and you're going to join an after-school club to meet people with similar interests.

3. Practice saying to yourself, "I'm excited about..." and "I'm going to...," adding in your positive outcome and actions.

Trust yourself

In order for our brains to grow and change, we have to challenge them. So if you're finding something difficult, that's a good thing! It's a really great opportunity to boost your brain and show yourself how putting in effort can help you do things that once seemed nearly impossible.

But sometimes we can feel scared of trying things that we think are too difficult. We might panic at the thought of even trying because we don't trust ourselves enough to believe we can succeed.

It's important to remember that just because you can't do something right now, it doesn't mean you'll never be able to. Were you born knowing how to talk, read, or write? No! But you tried and practiced over and over, and you got there in the end.

If you're feeling a bit panicked about a new challenge, it can help to remember a list of past successes. Those might be times when you've changed a habit, learned something new, or taken on a responsibility.

Write a list with all the examples you can think of. Think about big steps throughout your life, such as learning to feed yourself, getting dressed, reading, writing, and so on.

Keep the list and look at it whenever you worry that you can't do something. The list shows that, with effort and practice, you can make huge changes.

Not a competition

Have you ever fallen behind a group, maybe because you stopped to tie your shoelaces, and then been shocked to see how far ahead they suddenly were?

You might also get this panicky feeling if it seems like you're falling behind others in your class. Or maybe you want to be the best, but feel like people are catching up to you.

Seeing people in a fixed order, with winners at the top and losers at the bottom, just isn't realistic or helpful. Worrying about our position in this order can make us feel competitive with everyone, and cause us to avoid challenges in case we "fail."

In reality, everyone's brain is always changing, so there is no fixed order. Some of the best ways to grow your brain are to take on new challenges and learn from others!

Jana

I always loved playing tennis at my local club, and I was the best player for my age. I guess I got used to being the "star."

But last year I noticed that one girl, Alexis, was getting way better. I used to be able to beat her without really trying, but I started winning by fewer and fewer points. Then, one day, she beat me in a match.

I panicked that maybe I wasn't good after all, and behaved really badly. I told people that Alexis had cheated, and then pretended to be sick to get out of playing the next week.

Then I talked to my dad, and he helped me see how it was a good thing that Alexis was challenging me. He showed me that I could learn from her and improve my own game. I said sorry to Alexis, and we have so much fun playing together now. We are both helping each other to improve!

13

Panic button

Have you noticed that when you're panicking, it feels like an alarm has gone off in your head? Just like when a real alarm goes off, it can be so shocking that it's hard to think clearly at first. Your head can feel full of noise, confusion, and worry. You might even feel sick or as though you can't breathe.

So what's going on when you feel this way? Well, your brain is very good at protecting you, but it can also overreact when it thinks you're in danger.

Your amygdala is a part of your brain that can react quickly to the world around you, and work with other parts of the brain to decide if you're in danger. If the answer is "yes," your brain hits the panic button!

If you need to escape a charging elephant, it's quite helpful for your brain to shout "Run! Quick! Now!" until you do it. It's not so helpful when the "danger" you're worried about is something like reading out loud in class…

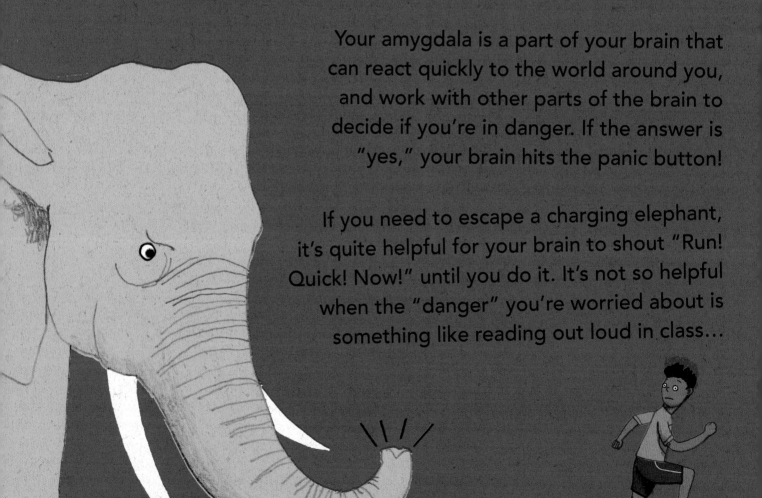

You know how you do fire alarm practices at school, so you know what to do in case of an emergency? Try practicing these ways to help your brain when it's hitting the panic button, but you aren't actually in danger.

1. Take 10 deep, slow breaths. Imagine your belly inflating like a balloon as you breathe in, and then gently deflating again as you breathe out.

2. Close your eyes and think of a place, a person or pet, and an activity that makes you feel happy and relaxed. Then, put them all together—so you might picture yourself singing on a beach with your cat!

3. Scrunch up your fingers and toes really tight and then let them relax. Start with one hand, then the other, and then your feet one at a time. You can also try hunching up your shoulders and then imagine them melting down your back like ice cream.

Remember to always let a trusted adult know if you feel panicky, sick, or like you can't breathe. You don't have to deal with these feelings alone.

Reach out

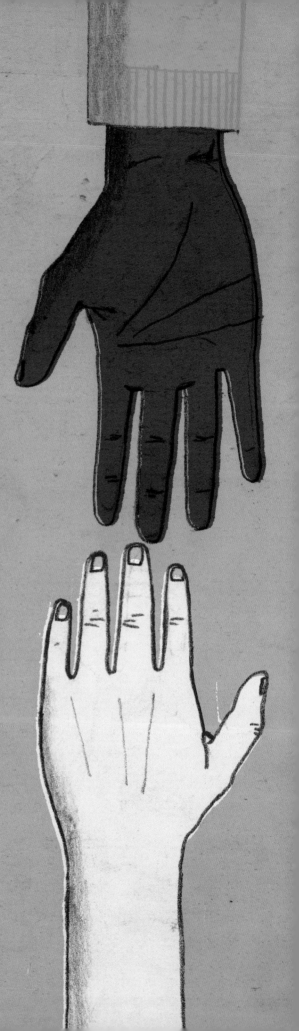

Although we can try a lot of different things to help us handle our worries, sometimes we also need to reach out and let other people help us.

Everyone feels worried and panicky sometimes, and we all know how difficult and horrible it can be. Sometimes, just telling someone about it can make us feel better and less alone.

Even if the adults in your life seem busy and stressed themselves, that doesn't mean they don't care about your problems. They just might not have noticed how difficult you're finding things. Adults can't read minds!

Ask a trusted adult about starting up regular **"Talk Time"** sessions, where you can take a few minutes to talk over anything that is worrying you.

It's best if these sessions are at a regular time, so no one forgets or ends up not having time to fit it in.

If you find it hard to remember things that upset you during the day, try writing them down in a small notebook. Take the notebook with you for Talk Time.

Keep a Talk Time diary of what you talk about during the sessions, and any plans you make for trying to help you with your worries. This will help you track how you're feeling and how the plans are working out for you.

Everything changes

Change is a part of life. The sun rises every day, but besides that almost everything else changes at some point. Change can be really difficult and even a little scary sometimes, especially if it's a big change, like moving to a new house or school.

It can make us panic about what will happen, and wish that everything could just stay the same. But we can't avoid change, so we have to work on how we react to it instead.

Luckily, our brains are always changing too—just like every part of our bodies, and everything else in nature. With some time and effort, we can help guide that change so that we end up feeling calmer and more positive about new and different situations.

Rodrigo

We moved to a new country last year and suddenly everything was different and strange. I had to go to a new school and learn a new language. It was all really difficult and scary.

I just wanted to go back home, and for everything to go back to how it was before. I missed my friends so much, and my aunt and cousins who lived just down the street. I felt like I'd never make friends here or do well at school and it made me feel really upset and panicky.

I talked to my parents about it and they completely understood. Moving was a big change for them too! They explained how they tried to focus on the positives and the new opportunities here. They were taking things one step at a time.

It was hard, but I started trying to do the same. I began keeping a diary of all the new things I was learning and doing. I'm much happier now and I've made some really nice friends! I still miss my old home sometimes, but I can now also see the good things about coming here.

DO YOUR RESEARCH

If you're feeling scared or stressed about doing something new, do some research to get more familiar with it first. It can help you feel more confident about taking on a new challenge.

For example, if you're starting swimming lessons, you could ask a trusted adult to help you find videos online that show you what to expect when learning to swim. You could also talk to friends who like swimming and ask them about it.

Maybe you're worried because you don't understand a new subject at school? Ask a trusted adult to help you look for fun books, activities, or videos that can give you some extra information on the subject. The best way to learn is when you are having fun!

Charlie

When my mom said we were going camping on our vacation, I felt really panicky about it. The only thing I knew about camping was that it meant sleeping in a tent, outside in the dark. I'm sometimes scared of the dark in my own bed, so I hated the idea of sleeping outside!

When I complained to my friend Aisha at school, she said that she loved camping. She went with her family every year, and they did really fun things like toasting marshmallows over a fire and singing songs.

My big sister had been camping, too, with her Girl Scouts club. She showed me pictures from her trip, and it did look kind of fun! She said a girl on the trip had brought a battery-powered night-light, and I could ask if our parents would get one for me.

Afterward, I felt better about going on the trip, and even got a little excited. In the end, I actually had a really good time camping—even though it rained a lot!

WHAT CAN I DO?

Sometimes you might worry about a lot of things at the same time, making it feel like there's a huge, dark storm cloud of worries hanging over you. It's not a nice feeling and it can make you panic because you don't know how to get rid of it.

Start by trying to pick out the different worries and talking with a trusted adult about how you could feel better about each one.

Some of your worries might be easier to deal with than others. For example, if you're worried about falling behind in class, you can talk to your teacher and parents and get some extra help.

But if you're worried about big things, such as climate change, you just can't solve that all by yourself.

It may make you feel a bit panicky to think about things in life that you can't control, but you can help your brain grow and change so it feels more comfortable with this idea.

Over time, you can learn to focus on what you can do to help, and accept that you might not be able to change certain things.

With the help of a trusted adult, make a **mind map** of your worries and what you can do to help make each one better. For bigger issues, such as climate change, think about how you can join with others to make a difference. Maybe you could write letters to people in power or raise money for a charity or organization.

For worries that you can't control, such as something bad happening to someone you love, talk about how that makes you feel and how the adults in your life could help you deal with these feelings.

what could go wrong?

When we are really worried about something, we can sometimes panic and imagine the worst possible outcome.

For example, if you're nervous about singing in a school show, you might convince yourself that you'll forget all the words and fall off the stage.

Your brain is trying to prepare you for the worst, but it's not being very helpful when it makes you even more nervous!

Try training your brain to focus on what is more likely to happen instead. Think about what actions you can take to make a positive outcome more likely. Practicing these things can help you feel much more confident and calm about new challenges.

Best outcome

Worst outcome

1. Think about something that you're worried about going wrong. What are the best and worst ways it could possibly turn out? Keep it realistic—no unicorns flying down to carry you away!

2. Draw a scale with the best and worst outcomes at either end. Talk with a trusted adult to fill in some "in-between" outcomes that are good, okay, or bad.

3. Decide together what you think is most likely to happen. Where on the scale is that? Talk about the actions you could take to push the most likely outcome further toward the "best" end. Then, put them into an action plan.

IF IT DOES GO "WRONG"

The reality is that sometimes things don't go quite as well as you might have hoped. It's a part of life and it happens to everyone. And actually, it can be much better for your brain than things turning out perfectly!

Scientific studies have shown that people learn more from making mistakes than from getting things right. When you make a mistake, special electrical signals spark in your brain and this appears to be linked to better learning over time.

Instead of panicking about making mistakes, think of them as great opportunities to grow your brain. It's time to get excited about making mistakes!

Look at the snakes and ladders board above—notice anything strange about it? There are ladders AND snakes in the same squares, because this is a special "brain-growing" version.

Think of the ladder as an "easy win," such as "I find a subject easy without having to study." Now think of the snake as the negative side, such as "I don't learn good study habits."

Next, try thinking of the snake as a "big mistake," such as "I got a lower mark than usual on my spelling test." The ladder could stand for a great learning opportunity, such as "I can learn how to use flash cards to practice spelling words I find tricky."

The point of the activity isn't to win or lose the game. It is to show how something that feels negative in the short term can be more positive in the long term—and the other way around!

Tomorrow is another day

When things happen that make you feel really bad,
it can sometimes seem like you'll never feel happy again.
If you think everything is ruined and there's no going back
to the way things were before, it is easy to start panicking.

But it's important to remember that everything changes
and nothing lasts forever. You've made it through difficult
things before, and gone from feeling bad to feeling happy
again. There's no reason that this time is any different.

Rather than panicking, try thinking about what you
can do to fix things or feel happier. What actions
could you take to make tomorrow better than today?

Chris

A couple of months ago, I got caught cheating on a test and the teacher lectured me in front of the whole class. I was so embarrassed, I didn't want to go back to school the next day. My stomach hurt just thinking about it.

I told my dad, and we talked about why I felt like I had to cheat and what I could do now to make things better. I admitted that I hadn't really been paying attention in class, and then during the test I panicked when I didn't understand the questions.

I made two "I'm sorry" cards to take in the next day—one for my teacher and one for my friend whose test I cheated from. I wrote a message in each card, explaining that I knew cheating was wrong and how I was going to do better in the future.

My dad and I made a plan to talk about my schoolwork every evening, and it's really helping me to stay focused and keep putting in effort.

29

REMEMBER: DON'T PANIC!

Read through these tips for a quick reminder of how best to avoid panicking!

Be a future friend to yourself. What can you do now to reduce your stress later?

If you feel nervous about a new challenge, try telling yourself you're excited about it instead.

Start regular Talk Time sessions with a trusted adult, where you can talk to them about your worries.

If you don't believe you can learn something new, make a list of the things you have already learned. They are proof you can!

If you're finding big changes difficult, talk with a trusted adult about what you can do to feel more positive.

Find out, and practice, what makes you feel calmer when your brain starts to panic.

Make a mind map of your worries with a trusted adult. Look at each one individually.

Remember that life isn't a competition. Focus on your own brain-growing journey.

If you're worried about trying something new, do some research into it first.

Don't be afraid of making mistakes—learning from them helps your brain grow!

Instead of worrying that the worst will always happen, talk with a trusted adult and decide together what's most likely to happen.

If you think you've behaved badly, don't panic. Think about how you can make it better tomorrow.

Glossary

fixed mindset   If you are using a fixed mindset, you believe that your intelligence is fixed and can't be changed

future friend   Being a "future friend" to yourself means taking actions now to help you avoid panic in the future

growth mindset   If you are using a growth mindset, you believe that your intelligence is always changing because your brain can grow stronger

mind map   A diagram with lines and circles for organizing information so that it is easier to remember

neurons   Cells in your brain that pass information back and forth to each another

Talk Time   Time that you put aside every day to talk with a trusted adult about anything that is worrying you

Index

Notes for adults

The concept of a "growth mindset" was developed by psychologist Carol Dweck, and is used to describe a way in which effective learners view themselves as being on a constant journey to develop their intelligence. This is supported by studies showing how our brains continue to develop throughout our lives, rather than intelligence and ability being static.

Responding with a growth mindset means being eager to learn more and seeing that making mistakes and getting feedback about how to improve are important parts of that journey.

A growth mindset is at one end of a continuum, and learners move between this and a "fixed mindset"—which is based on the belief that you're either smart or you're not.

A fixed mindset is unhelpful because it can make learners feel they need to "prove" rather than develop their intelligence. They may avoid challenges, not wanting to risk failing at anything. This reluctance to make mistakes—and learn from them—can negatively affect the learning process.

Help children develop a growth mindset by:
- Giving specific positive feedback on their learning efforts, such as "Well done, you've been practicing…" rather than non-specific praise, such as "Good effort" or comments such as "Smart girl/boy!" that can encourage fixed-mindset thinking.
- Sharing times when you have had to persevere with learning something new, and what helped you succeed.
- Encouraging them to keep a learning journal, where they can explore what they learn from new challenges and experiences.
- Helping them understand that they haven't done anything wrong if they do feel panicky, but that it's not a nice feeling and that's why we work on developing positive habits to try to avoid it.